the first shall be

the last shall be

the first and last

in the parting

in the middle

in the joining

rning towards

the glance ahead

turning back to

the lost moment

the remembrance

ong dotted lines. Attach BB to CC. Hold both ends of strip and give one end half a turn. Attach DD to AA.

A

turning we all   we all retire askew   turning they all   they all are joined anew   turning the last   the last or first

A

the present moment   the appearance   the absence then   the faces separate   the faces joined   the faces are the face

Dealing with the edge

By the same author:
pebbles, debris and other poems (2003)

Dealing with the edge

Jim Dening

Arcade Publishers
2016

Dealing with the edge: first published 2011 by Arcade Publishers, The Tannery, The Frith, Ledbury HR8 1LW, UK. Second edition with corrections published 2016.

Text typeset in Garamond 12pt, titles in 18pt italic.

Printed on acid-free long life paper and bound in England by Orphans Press, Leominster HR6 0LD, UK.

A catalogue record for this book is available from the British Library. ISBN 978-0-9560714-3-9

Contents

Poems follow alphabetically by title because the poet gave up trying to arrange the sequence in a deeply sensitive way.

... too much i' the sun

After visiting Olafur Eliasson's 'Weather Project' at the Tate Modern

No purpose after all
only the instinctive tendency
we take our hopeful
our pretentious steps
towards the warmth
before the unknown time will come
and loose our grip upon the rail
nothing is present at the centre
an imagined voice
nurtured over centuries
claiming authority
until baffled by sleep
or by desire
a trick of language
legends of revelation
justifying power
for years I thought if only
we can bring attention
to the unconscious life
this will shift the universe
or a fraction of a fraction
of an ounce of it
against the grain
towards the idea
we were too much i' the sun
complacent desperate
our young earth growing
crack'd and dessicated
what chance did we ever have
to look into the dark
once blinded by the light?

15 February 2003

A river of people flows uphill
past the ancient common shrines
of justice medicine art and science
and seething presses its hot body
against the pillars of parliament
as if there were the slightest chance
of a barge's passing turbulence
cracking the embankment of the capital.
In bulging tidal waves of noise
frozen for a deafening moment
everybody stands mouth wide and howls.
Bitter unity and good intent
converging from a thousand towns
like water running over stones.

A kind of silence

If somehow you achieve it
the end of childish things
it is hard to do without
the confiding and self-pity
expecting people to listen
to your preoccupations
in easy talk over drinks
in resonant restaurants
and the worst indulgence of all
using your own children
for reassurance or approval;
on the new side turning
reluctantly from the past
assembling the fruit of years
by an effort of will
into self-reliance and solitude;
it is like passing through an air-tight door
no it is like closing the electric sunroof
when travelling at speed
there is a long hiss and a plonk
followed by a kind of silence.

At a concert in Mellor Church

It wasn't sleep
although my eyes were closed
finding the music too urgent
to pretend conventional attention
I let go of where I sat and cast off
in a boat seized and hoist by waves
hauled headlong away
the church a vessel on moving waters
new currents rising from below.

Outside among the tombs
I have just kindly warmed
the grave of some old soul
the glittering city spread wide
as far as each horizon
vain mirror of the galaxy
the dim church marooned
against the night a hulk perched
upon its mound like Noah's ark
faint light at narrow windows
waves receding.

A wreath of smoke
i.m. Richard Trench, d. 1997

We should have seen it coming
or looked for the look in his eye
which one day must have passed
the unknown notch separating
the lively from the dying
after that it seems a kind of slide
we despise the machine
but in the mechanical
our life and death are passed
our thoughts being vapour
emitted by the inexorable
self-terminating process
we sat in the garden with
your psychedelic rabbit
three days before but where was
the click in the system
the change of rhythm
a sound a smell a colour
a flicker of a nerve in the little finger
a shiver in the leaves of the tree
behind you as you smiled
in a faint wreath of smoke
when we sat in the garden
three days before. We resented you
amid the pity of it
for leaving without warning
as if we have to keep practising
the same sense of loss.

Communion
for Mo and Ève

Around the kitchen table
already dark outside
we are concentrating
an hour passes by
silence resonates
tiny sounds burst in
normally unheard such as
the brush on paper
an escape of breath
as you purse your lips
frowning at the things
before you on the table
things in a different
category of being
such as a glass of wine
not to be drunk
a slice of bread
not to be devoured
now your hair is moving
on your shoulder
something is about to happen
out of the silence
deafening noises
papers are moved
the brush is rinsed
a chair pushed back
I am filling glasses
with wine we can drink
we will take the painting
to our friend tomorrow
hoping the quiet picture
of bread and wine
on our kitchen table
will make her whole again.

Dealing with the edge

This not this is a wooden board
which has been painted on the front;
in a worked and scraped-off blue
representing notionally a table top
less feasibly an ocean
on which a ghostly beer mug
unperspectived floats;
beside an intended ashtray
bearing a faint fag pluming smoke
curled by a finger in the paint;
and down a bit not far away
there is a small round shape
a void a moon a lime
because it needed green;
along the sides Arscott the artist
has laid a heavy swathe
of streaky whitish colour
limiting the supposed table
and its nebulous objects.
He says it is his way
of dealing with the edge.

Declaring it a fig

In January in the middle of a field
relieved by thaw a man is digging holes,
on Monday morning, first things first this week.
The work makes warm, his coat and woolly hat
hang at the centre on the walnut tree.
He has paced it out around this middle point
and at the measured spots the holes appear
with former inside earth now piled outside.
Then to the edges of the field he goes
seeking markers in the old dead grass
where oak tree seedlings spring;
dig patiently and tease the taproot free,
the anchor and the mirror of the tree,
explaining to each one why it must move.

The small trees are sitting in new places now,
he practises his scheme. From number one
he walks the unseen line to number four.
He walks one four two and eight five seven,
then back to one. Older trees if watching
will be amused by this, he thinks, and laughs.
Then sees again the central walnut tree
he planted by mistake ten years before,
for some reason misinformed,
and meant to plant the Buddha tree: a fig.
How would a fig tree flourish in the frost?
Let the walnut stay, ceremonially
we will declare it is a fig. Next day
the field was shriven by the frost again,
he wanted to to encourage his new trees,
stood with them in their circle motionless.

Dee pwang

You told me I had something to make up to you
you rested your hand on my knee in the pub
you looked in my eyes very gravely and loving
I knew what you meant I felt the same
we remembered the debt from last time
the delectable scrambled intimacy
so tender in so little time and space
you trembled and bit your lip and half smiled
we had to carry it away with us.

In the luxury of discussion we decide
such unfulfilment is unacceptable between
lovers such as us though in the circumstances
unusual and extenuating the judges award
dee pwang for determination but for artistic merit
alas nul pwang we laugh out loud at the memory.
Now we are making it up to each other
now in rapt attention we receive each other
your body round mine begins to deliquesce
your gaze flickers in the transience of our lives.

Don't worry about your dad

Don't worry about your dad
he is learning to be free
it will take exactly all his life
plus a bit borrowed from
the hours of inertia when
nothing fruitful was conceived;
if you think he's left it late
to refine the fragile inner self
remember he was a journalist
and always likes a deadline best.
Ten days late for his own birth
and ever since has scurried round
assembling ideas into little piles
lacking the patience it requires
to make a papier-mâché monument;
he will of course be present at his end,
will try not to arrive too soon
but could well be late frequently
delayed by words and fantasies;
as awake as it is given him to be
and as prepared as skimpy readings
hurried exercises meagre charity
and wishful thinking will allow;
if by himself he sleeps and hasn't
set the alarm he'll need your help
so wake him up! remembering
there is a limit to the child's attempt
to save a parent in extremis
from the parent's personal consequence;
this is just his note reminding you
to laugh at things and laugh at him
let famous irony console him now
in case he doesn't realise any more
that things are not as serious as they seem.

This flippancy comes from sadness
or the fear of sadness like a tinge
upon the childhood vision of his parents' lives:
all that was unexpressed therein,
anxiety leaking out ahead of joy,
love ensnared in obligation, lives
derived from older lives and unrenewed;
the family conspired against bad news
and made a shelter out of sentiment:
no one died, they went; and no one died
but they were good in retrospect:
in life the hapless and the feckless
were unforgiven till they fell sick and went
and were reclassified as good;
a generation later I grieve still,
and dream my father comes, and we embrace,
because we were unsatisfied:
we awaited his and my release;
what flows from him and gathers force in me
I transmit and through these words transform
so you in your essences may be free:
you will not be your father's father
nor I my children's child.

Lean upon him while he is robust,
grasp the unformed memories of today;
who will tell of the weaker part
behind the brave and glamourised façade?
Your dad has strapped ideas on him like wings:
he is learning how to fly,
oh yes, running up and down
waving his arms and weeping with joy;
unlike poor Icarus, victim of bad science,

he dare not fly too near the sun.
Who will tell of the absurdities and drink
and delectable excursions with women
insofar as anybody knows: such things,
he used to say, are neither here nor there.
But pain, such as his father's deforming pain,
or any commonplace humiliating pain,
would see off bravura soon enough
and wreck the calm philosophy
of perfumed skins and quiet nights.

Wheel me into the sun;
uncork the wine;
it is here and now the kingdom
if it can be seen or grasped;
yes, it is quite like coming
to a woman much desired:
it is preoccupying and
perhaps illusory even if
it seems to be given to us;
like waves advancing
events have a way
of happening as they must,
but I can throw a pebble if I want
into the breaking wave.

Dubious trip

the first shall be
the last shall be
the first and last
in the parting
in the middle
in the joining
in the turning
turning towards
the glance ahead
turning back to
the lost moment
the remembrance
the present moment
the appearance
the absence then
the faces separate
the faces joined
the faces are the face
turning we all
we all retire askew
turning they all
they all are joined anew
turning the last
the last or first

Dying echo
prompted by an incident in Andrzej Wajda's film Kanal

Wading in fumes along a sewer,
aspiring towards a distant glow,
blurred lines coming into focus;
finding a river flowing calmly past,
willows waving by the further bank;
transfixed behind an iron grill,
arms spread out in cross, knuckles white,
holding feet above the slime;
a small boat with water rat and mole
rows by, the sun slants down through leaves,
ripples on the surface dazzle;
the dying echo of a flute arrives.

Easter Day

And he took bread, and when he had given thanks,
he brake it, and gave to them, saying,
this is my body which is given for you:
this do in remembrance of me...

There was a thick white frost along the lane,
the birds still mute with cold inside the hedge;
but surely it was dark at such an hour,
or is memory at fault? Those years ago
there were three communions before nine o'clock,
on Christmas Day at least; meanwhile the boy
leaps shivering from his bed and on his bike
towards the church. This lasted for a year or so.
Throughout his life he felt upon his scalp
the touch, slight pressure, pause, removal
of the bishop's hand; how serious the boy,
his catechism well prepared, kneeling
in his own cathedral, his own city;
and how moved, in all his later years,
by the slow sad words of the ceremony,
the primitive symbolic sacrament,
the acknowledgment of others as oneself,
the continuity amid mortality.

Eventually, one Easter Day,
a red sun tried to shine upon the world,
a russet colour in the tight closed buds,
with a fine frost set hard along the road,
a dust of snow in fields on either side;
he sets off scarfed and gloved upon his bike,
the whole year's thoughts assemble in his head
and just before the church he says out loud:
 – Honestly I cannot go in there,
I have to try a different way
even if I miss the breaking of the bread
the slow sad words of the communion
and the laying on of hands;

another time I'll nod my head politely
to Colonel this and Mrs that,
but not for appearances or even for
forgiveness will I go in there today
and kneel beside them at the altar rail,
adding to the row of upturned soles
imagining the row of upturned souls
and humbly shuffle back towards my pew
eyes downcast and holy for another week.
Let me ride instead in chastening air
and search for silence and solitude
offered like a gift upon my head
to replace the imprint of the bishop's hand
and wonder whether sad persuasive words
are just a lure to obedience and belief ...

With such comical and ceremonious words
the adolescent seriously addressed himself,
marking the end of childhood in his mind;
and so rode out along the crackling lanes
towards a different kind of holy place
an ancient chapel long disused,
remote and solitary among the fields,
with mossy stones and empty presence;
feeling his questions should be attended to
he stopped and looked about;
he stopped and looked about.

Embracing the cello
in homage to Miklós Perényi*

He sidles on, he tiptoes,
it is a diffidence,
he carries the cello in front of him,
it hides him almost.

He is sitting arms and legs akimbo
as we could well imagine
some great ape embrace a tree;
his knees are spread apart,
the body of the cello lies between his thighs,
its neck reclines against his breast;
his shoulders are hunched around it,
his arms hang massively upon it,
his hands and fingers move
upon its surface while he waits.

His head is bent against the strings,
almost on the cello's shoulder,
he is gazing at the ground,
he is enfolded like a nutshell
before it ripens and then cracks apart,
the bow hangs loosely in his hand
while he waits upon his entry;
and suddenly he is playing, an instant
of tension and release as inevitable
and smooth as snow discarded by a leaf.

He is in a slow and sonorous space,
he leans as if he wanted to conceal
the secret places where the sound is born.
At last there is a sense of resolution –
his shoulders open and his head is freed –
his arms and fingers dart towards the notes
and now his face turns upward: his eyes
are seeing what we will hear; a smile has touched
the corner of his mouth like light,
and we have witnessed an ascent.

** after a performance of the Dvořák cello concerto
in the Bridgewater Hall, Manchester, April 2006.*

Faint light

Waking in the middle of the night
no light yet at the window
it is always nearly three o'clock
because I was born at three perhaps
the body is lying taut and dull
like the off-peak mechanism it is
full of stuff functioning for the moment
and sooner or later will be handled
or examined by unknown people
tipped and loaded and discharged
and burnt; through the ribs
and jaws and eyes will pour the fire
until remnants are raked and pounded
and tipped again just as once I let
the bony fragments of my mother's dust
slip through my fingers. Oh absurdity,
who could be afraid of nothing?
Self-contempt, fatigue
and the desire to sleep
turn me towards her warmth
a faint light at the window now.

Green man

Consider this photo of a tree
(contained within a poem):
an oak in winter symmetry,
the statement of its strength,
an intricacy of twiggery,
balance, solitude,
magnificence, or is there falsity
in the crafted silhouette,
the centering in the frame,
the idealised monument.

I have grown inside a tree
a green man risen from the earth,
feet planted on the ground, an aura
of energy tingling on the skin,
leaves growing at the fingertips,
a crowd of creatures in my arms;
as the perishing of age invades
the superficial symmetry,
the picture of the tree will fade away
and sentimental memories decay.

Hapless

A sort of mania
to take in everything
remember all things
taught or heard or seen
such vanity understandable
in a child secure
in the childhood space
touching everything
and round the house
inspecting cupboards
reading parental books
trying to understand
what is not explained;

it continues through life
cannot be assuaged
we should be grateful
for such slight torment
such curiosity but
what do we do with it
what is it really for
shall we give it
to our children
like a permanent itch;

even if not rocking
or washing our hands
compulsions rule us
we are the slaves
of small forms of order
take the absurdity
of eating a biscuit
the right way up
or even noticing
it has a top as if
it might stay that way

inside us and emerge
digested discarded yet
upright to the end
as we were told to be;

things are more serious than this
I used to try to stand
my empty trousers up
beside the bed
to jump straight into
in the morning
not to attack the day
but to see if I could
now I read the paper
obsessively all through
nodding and cursing
feeling the warm trickle
of outrage or dissent
the hollow trousers
of complacent impotence
are standing waiting
as usual for tomorrow;

believe in nothing
maybe we'll discover
something decent later
remember all we know
we take on trust
from words of others
absurdity is preferable
to persuasion or untruth
the best teacher
is disinterested
tells the pupil go:
test it for yourself.

Heavenly vision

One sunny morning we lay late in bed
and saw to our surprise a light, like flame
alive upon the ceiling, intersected
by the lattice of the window frame.

– Of course! we said, it is the sun reflected
from the stream into our room above;
and when we looked again the patch had moved
as if to measure the passage of much love.

The sun rose further, and just above the bed
a human figure passed across the patch
refracted upside down. – Of course! we said,
it is a passer-by upon the bridge.

But on the bridge a crowd had stopped to stare
down at the glassy surface of the stream
whereon a vision shimmered like the secret dream
of mystic union of a heavenly pair;
the people marvelled, giving praise out loud,
until the sun went in behind a cloud.

In Brandenburg forest

The music stands are high today
no chairs are waiting on the stage
the players are standing up to play.

When strong winds invade a forest
the dancing works down from each crest
the very trunks of trees will sway.

The double bass leans into the gale!
the fiddles heave their scurrying stave
the trembling flute is blown aside.

The players shift their roots to found
a better balance on the ground
against the tempest felt inside.

In the borderlands

Beside old roads you see them,
the ditch and bank of other times,
the deer park of an ancient hundred,
the tribal boundary,
a claim of sovereignty
intended to contain and to exclude;
the struggling sweating men long dead,
their sharp defences overgrown,
their fallen earthworks fading in the mist,
the echoes of their voices all but gone.
– I had another sheepdog once, see?
came a voice along the bar:
he ran off on Offa's Dyke one day,
in a place where rustling aspen grow
so thick you're not sure where you are.
I heard him in the bushes growl and bark,
the wind was blowing strong and sharp
and turning over every silver leaf;
up flew the birds, all you saw of them
was rooks far-flung around the sky.
I heard the bark turn into a whimper
and my old dog come limping back
his leg all bloody and fur a-clotted,
I could tell from looking in his eye
he'd seen a thing invisible to me;
with the wind increasing all the time
I seemed to hear men's voices shouting
and footsteps running and the clash of iron;
with the aspen lashing all the time,
a whirring in the air, a flying branch
or something heavy whacked me to the ground,
my shoulder took a vicious twinge;
I thought it high time to be out of there
and back here for a pint and living company.
My old dog was always quiet after that,
he'd look at me sidelong and anxious-like.

In the county hospital

They have the records
my records are in Manchester
I was writing a poem
almost finished
when they brought me here
my number is 24
I was at Cambridge
my records exist
yes my name is Dulcie
my cousin was called
was called
he died before me
I saw the pope
upon the Malvern Hills
he had red shoes
that is why
they put me in here

In the maze

Walking the labyrinth inlaid
in the cathedral floor
at Chartres or Saint-Quentin
quickly drawn within
all but to the centre
(why not transgress and overstep)
then borne as quickly out
and round the periphery.

This is like running a finger
upon a sharpened blade
the palace of the king was called
the palace of the double axe
now circumnavigate
one hemisphere towards the other
a kind of spiral on an axis
a slow giration inward.

Supposedly love spun the thread
she also gave the sword
shouldering the heavy skein
he steps out of the light
into dimming corridors
rough and dirty where the stench
and an attenuated echo roll
from the centre forth in waves.

How simply destined heroes slay
the half-seen half-man half-beast
they are the casual instruments
the cleansing agents sent
by the mind into the mind
but memories of the slain
still linger in the pathways
stained with their residue.

In the underground

Who has arranged all this behind my back?
a party rolling up in a railway carriage,
old-style, but spacious, yellow-lit,
a little dim perhaps at either end.
Here comes mother, smiling, in her apron,
bringing one of her apple pies, and dad
carrying a box of tomatoes and runner beans,
oh, dad! in your gardening trousers as usual,
grandma is having her seventh cup of tea
and there a little fellow watching,
shy, no taller than the sideboard.
A kind of mist descends and all
are rendered silent and motionless.

There must have been a whistle,
an unheard signal from the stationmaster,
the carriage is slowly shunted off
into a tunnel, where it dwindles,
still yellow-lit, to a little point far off.
From up the line –which is up and which is down? –
from the other side another carriage comes!
Another party going on on board!
Oh, I remember her, and her, and now
some station names appear through the glass –
Sèvres-Babylone goes slowly by,
and slowly a sad face has turned away.
Surely here is merriment, a dear friend
is pouring me Jack Daniels in a ritual way.

Now there is my pal, I will introduce my friends,
he is always oily, I shake his wrist.
Hiya, mate, he says. We look at one another.

The carriage jolts; you'd better get off, mate, he says.
The silent whistle blows, the party is swallowed up.
Out of the window, looking back at me
and waving are two small children and their dog.
This is too much! waiting on the platform –
here comes a repair wagon, all blank and closed,
it trundles slowly in and slowly passes by.
I can see inside, it is piled high with junk,
I can see my furniture and books and papers,
there is my armchair, perhaps I can jump in
while it's moving if I run hard now.

I was assembling

I was assembling the bits and pieces
the resolutions the sheets of paper
things to do or answer on the left
letters for posting on the right
and a clear space in front of me –
that's it! a clear space in front of me.

The unread books in several piles
the new arrivals hiding older ones
until I shuffle them not daring
to dump some unread stuff unread;
sometimes angrily I can cram
a half-read book into the shelves.

I was going to go through old ideas
and copy the best aphorisms
but I have been sorting my nice new
French squared-paper notebooks
according to size and colour.
I was assembling the rubbish neatly
to make a clear space in front of me
when I died.

Journey from Beirut to Damascus

Near the ruined heart the long street begins
a curving sword slices the city
this road was the green line
behold a building infected with destruction
a house engraved with a hundred bullet holes
foolish to walk into your front room
wise to crawl on hands and knees
now grass grows lizards dwell in fallen architecture
our friend writes Arabic in my notebook:
'the crying on the ruins' –
this is the Arabishi way, he says.

Swooping in a Syrian ex-New York city yellow cab
inspecting the landscape for biblical signs
here are chicanes a roadblock militias peering at us
children of the hizbollah offering sweets to mark a suicide
we had a tedious time of it with visas at the border
the only conversions on the road have been from dollars
surely we will know when we arrive.

In the old city its name borrowed for damask or damascene
near the statue of Saladin a crowd follows
a strange figure a man nine feet tall
I hope he will begin to preach but he is sad
in my dictionary I find the word for stilts
in case he is not a giant among men
my neighbour nods and grins we shake hands
he is offering small green bitter fruit
politely I eat one and shake his hand again.
In the street called straight we make friends
not for a few dollars or a coffee pot
but for the long look into the eyes
and the strange exchange of dignity.

At night returning to Beirut sticky
after handling objects and touching people
walking in the ruined heart rebuilt
with glistening arcades and cafe terraces
the ruins just behind are left unlit
a minister arrives men crowd to shake his hand
old militias take to money and authority
this district is known as Downtown now
the word is used in Arabic unchanged.

Journey to Relleu

Relleu is a small town of pre-Roman origin in south-eastern Spain

1 (The journey south)

Always beginning again
it has taken so long
arriving in the wrong place
other people seemingly ahead
while somewhere down the road
are sunlight warmth the best ideas
longing to combine flesh with spirit
by instinct we look towards the sun
cannot gaze upon its eye
blinking at the after-image
following the masters of knowledge
in uncertainty.
Spurning absurdity let us wait
with the patience of animals
and see only what we have to see
hear only what we have to hear;
the wagtail picks its flickering flight
neither learnt nor understood, but done;
the cat spares movement when it walks
ignores attention if attention
is a waste of time; we call this
the excellence of nature.

2 (The slipperiness of the city)

On the esplanada at Alicante
we walk upon the waves of the sea
the city is full of swirls and holes
my eyes and ears of commotion
all that is asked for is paid for
the comforts are too great
here we will stick fast

in the sociable embrace
of placid afternoons.
Only in memory or hope
is all luminous and speedy.
The museum hangs images
of strange distractions:
an unknown worthy of the city
gazing from his dark interior;
the hopeful saint half-kneeling
in the harmless wilderness
gazing on the absolute;
a woman rapturous in flight
from an unseen ravisher on the left
outside the picture frame
towards another on the right.

3 (The terraces on the hillside)

The ancient terraces from antiquity
decayed and inviting
form a kind of ladder
as far as the slope can go,
failing only at the precipice;
like points on railways
there are junctions and divisions
oblique connexions
side tracks and dead ends;
I was on one of these
yesterday or any other day
and see the figure over there
the neighbour or the brother I never had
in the mist of memory
gliding on a slender ledge
supported by elaborate walls
a long array of flat stone faces
features washed off by rain
the very life squeezed out of them.

4 (The stations of the cross)

We never thought of testing
how the pendulum might react
before each station of the cross;
violently it had swung
beside each terrace end
along an old decultivated slope
suggesting a change of force
a renewal of the wave
a memory of water
along the contour.
Testing what test of faith?
Who needs to know for sure
where waves of devotion have unfurled
or in what fervent spirit
the soldiers' faces were defaced
or where the bearers stumbled
and the crowd cried out
but recovering kept the monstrance
from touching earth
or if the lame threw off their crutches
or if a voice was heard within a cloud
that rested like a space ship at the top?
Or other voices asking would the bar
be open when we all came down?

5 (The forest of words)

Behind the red door
within the ancient arch
a father takes his teenage son
to see his woman friend,
she will help the boy.
It is what many men might wish
their fathers would have done for them.
Presently the boy skips home,
he will tell his mates tomorrow;

the father goes back the narrow way,
round the shadowy ravine
through the plantation
where the almond trees murmur
and words lie fallen on the ground.
The leaves are thick,
the sun arrives in snatches –
he trips upon a root,
stumbles, puts out a hand;
when he gets home
he finds almonds in his pocket
and unknown words
are rising in his mind.

6 (The ruined castle)

By the garage corner on the wall
there is a convex angle mirror
meant to help a vehicle emerge;
by accident you sometimes see
the ruined castle on the hill
caught in the mirror upside down
as if it had moved and posed,
performed a clever trick
just to attract attention;
no point in shuffling to it on your knees
or pushing a pea up with your nose
it is not a holy place
merely a relic of violence
with battlements reverting
to the rubble they once were;
a thousand pilgrims
pushing a thousand peas
would not transcend its lowliness.

7 (The ghosts of friends)

If we could learn to switch
the focus of our eyes
along the road we would behold
our old companions;
we think we hear their voices
but they are as a stone rolling
a dog barking
the leaves whispering;
we glimpse their shades flitting
in the riffles and puffles of the bushes.
There comes one, he was the last to go
of my friends he is wrapped up
around his heart and guts
where it went wrong for him
now he is drifting off
he was always avid
he used to have a lot to say
I can't make out his words.
While I am in this place
I will go and fetch my father
I have so much to tell him
he cannot be far away.

8 (The sun sends light into the ravine)

From the castle top they say
a secret staircase descends to the ravine,
to that very archway over there,
and in the passage are exactly
one thousand and one steps;
it would be hard to follow now
the tunnel has parted in the middle
the two ends inside have whipped away
like snakes in dusty earth
to silent caverns filled with stones;
in any case you cannot start,

the entrances are blocked
with tedium and indifference.
Go on scrabbling at the door –
decay, disuse make powerful bolts,
and mind your foothold or
the crumbling earth will yield
and dump you in rocks and brambles
bruised and bleeding scrambling
to get back where you began.
Allow the mounting sun
to warm your skin
and heal your hurt
and dry the ground;
as the work goes on,
hold still at transient noon, for then
you have no shadow.

Laugh at it

When one of my little family
had a cold or pain or bruise,
I would say in kindly tone:
know what you should do? Laugh at it!
I meant it well enough, but they,
through gritted teeth or watering eyes,
didn't want such good advice
from me when I was feeling fine.
I had in mind that laughing at things
detaches you from pain,
permits the ironic space,
prompts the immune system:
so I heard, or so I liked to think.
In our house, along the years,
it became a catchword and a kind of joke,
this so-called humorous advice.

The grasshopper has sung all summer,
the ant has stored up grain;
the merry one now asks for help:
eh bien, replies inexorably the ant, dansez maintenant!
I thought this funny once, until one day
I was suffering a woeful depression
of my own invention; the voice
of one who loved me once said:
now laugh at it yourself!
I tried but it was hard,
I murmured ha ha inside myself
to let in healing light and space,
but only a thin smile came
and no shifting the hard lump.
I woke up eventually because enough's enough;
things might not be funny
but I am going to jump about
as dancing shifts things round, and then we'll see.
I'll tell the fabulist if it is not too late
the wise may also be compassionate.

Lights out
after Cavafy

The people are gathering in groups on the street
they are waiting to hear the good news from abroad
their leader is fighting the forces of darkness.

Demonstrators are sending petitions to parliament
ambassadors and bishops have spoken in protest
their leader is fighting the forces of evil.

The people are emptying the shops of provisions
buying pizza and lager to last out the crisis
their leader is fighting the forces of terror.

A report has come in from a distant frontier
where an army of god put a town to the sword
but none were our people no names were reported.

A minister speaks with the blazing conviction
of people who dare not show doubt or inaction
but the sound is turned down as we heard it before.

Intellectuals criticise public hypocrisy
urging anti-imperial and humanist discourse
the government declines to accept their advice.

The people are frowning at flickering pictures
a news flash replaces the penalty shoot-out
our leader is pleased to have found a new enemy.

A power cut strikes and the screens all go blank
but the people are fetching their candles and blankets
and beer to make love in the welcoming darkness.

Like criticising a hammer

When a word strikes cleanly home
the other person feels the impact
and fills up with instant shock
quivering like a timber struck
or wavelets fleeing to the edge
even if the target is not the person
but an idea or a piece of work.

The other day I said to our friend:
– *il faut carrément casser le carrelage*,
meaning he must smash his recent work
and start again; we were in an impasse
of poor fit and poor decisions,
even so there was nothing personal,
the statement was obvious and correct.

He was silent, staring, acknowledging
the force and meaning of the words
if not the concussive consonants,
realising he was unable to disagree,
and taking the impact personally
would be like criticising a hammer.

Love poem anger poem
i.m. Janet Allen, d. March 2003

You wont read this
love poem anger poem
to you and your city
the two being once inseparable
now life has gone from vital places
your ghost is thinner
than the vapor from the gratings
round West 86th Street
or by the crossing to the park
where people are waiting with their dogs
the road is wet and black
I wouldnt want to cross there now
or upstairs at Panarellas
which has changed its name since then
or by the brown fronted bookstore
which has closed down altogether
you wont read this Janet
who could say there ought to be
a celebration of a life
when the truth is wretched
and desperate and wont turn back
I would blow the words towards you
like a cloud of dust
like your miserable ashes
if you were anywhere.

We were art lovers sure enough we
aspired to higher things
as well as lower we were
inspired by Kandinsky we
perspired on the spiral ramp
having marched sternly up
we used to slither down
more a glissade
than a promenade
poor Kandinsky
hardly got a look in

let alone his trousers felt
your hand arriving round
one of those fat pillars
and I if I could would tweak
your summer halter top
till at the bottom thirsty
from so much art and craft
we sucked strawberry soup
in the old-time restaurant.

Leaving on a cross-town street
which rapidly submerges in the park
and delivers past 5th Avenue toward
FDR drive and the Triboro bridge
where I used to turn to gaze across
and there it is the city skyline
the whole panoply as they say
glowing in the late afternoon
complex and incomprehensible
you cant get it in a glance
but it stays with you like a postcard
moments before the distraction
of all this magnificence
I had looked back for an instant
as the cab curved away into the park
and she still stood on that corner
tears streaming down her face
people round her with their dogs
waiting for the lights to change.

At the Cooper Hewitt by chance
cant remember why we went
no doubt to see Julia Cameron
or Ansel Adams or perhaps
your friend Ruthie's photographs
of shiny straining athletes or
her lesser work on smiling dogs
we found on the museum step
an army an array well ten at least

of eggs all standing on their ends
students were standing eggs on end
eggs were standing round
upon their broader ends
sometimes slightly swaying
we were attracted by this egg sample
and wondering if I could excel too
like doubting Thomas I took an egg
and found it also stood for me
it was noon on March the 21st
as time moved on past one o'clock
the eggs subsided on their sides
I have a photograph as proof.

Eventually a recorded voice kept saying
this number has been disconnected
this number has been disconnected
where was I on March 2nd
or in the days before enwrapt
in trivial concerns
I have come for no good reason
to check your places out
here is a woman
in the corner coffee shop
she is serving me
not far from where you lived
a small vein is ticking
in her forehead
she is doubtless fine
her face is tender
her skin will be warm
whoever she may be
she is an example
of how easy it should be
to be a living woman
but it is no good
the people are blank
the streets are blank
some kind of mirror
is departed from the city.

Mozart's number

I met a woman many years ago,
after a concert we spoke a word or two –
she may well be still alive,
I have seen no notice otherwise;
not beautiful but quiet and collected,
a musician and so containing beauty.
At the time I didn't know about it,
she wasn't holding up her arm in any way,
I saw the numbers printed on her wrist
like kids jot telephone numbers,
but neat and square and almost straight
and slightly blurred around the edges.
They say that Mozart saved her,
as if to mean she lived when others died,
as if by privilege; but none of us is saved,
for all our gifts, except by chance.

New howl

Here it comes again it will wash all over us
will we get to the high ground in time
the moral high ground ha ha
or just to the kitchen and make a cup of tea
in the company of like-minded friends
otherwise here it comes all of it all over again
the smile the patient fervent exposition
telling us things we want when we don't want them
patronising with paternalistic platitude
unless we escape or refuse or ripost
you remember the account of inmates with aphasia
watching tv and roaring with laughter
at a political speech they understood not a word
but grasped the body language perfectly
we see performances like this each day
these are public voices communicating with us
they have been elected they like to say
as if that legitimizes nonsense
presuming to communicate with us
us the noble confused inarticulate people
why should we suffer foolish ideas
or obfuscation and hypocrisy
let us seize on something better and talk about it
diversity and friendship is that what it might be
recognition and general will is that what it might be
since common sense and truthfulness too much to hope for
who would care about the drivel if in some other sense
we had a reasonable best or knew a way towards it
or even could express it in ready terms
who would care about the absurd language of power
coined by excited lackeys writing speeches in back rooms
if there were refuge unless things too far gone for refuge
there is only blockage and bafflement along the streets
fine sentiments are cheap and plentiful like human life
the consequences of mediocrity are all around
in resignation we know it we protest we lament

No wonder we sit staring into space

No wonder we move our lips in unspoken sentences or rehearsals of self-defence

No wonder we jump up and walk towards a half-read book then look for scissors to trim a finger nail or pour a glass of wine and gaze at it surprised

No wonder we walk round shopping malls fingering empty unbought clothes

No wonder we put out nuts for birds and stand there giving little whistles with arms outstretched as if St. Francis

No wonder we watch atrocities and violence and hurricanes and forest fires on tv

No wonder we steer our motors through public spaces like rafts in a cascade

No wonder we walk on ancient landscapes ignoring the bodies of people rendered dust beneath our feet

No wonder we burrow into warm bodies smelling welcoming folds and hollows

No wonder we have given up on certainty

No wonder we sit up late watching flames licking over logs and turning them to ash

No wonder we write unpublished letters to the newspaper asking if the divinity has noticed anything unusual recently

No wonder we talk to our friends and laugh and feast and celebrate

No wonder we look strangers in the eye and shake their hand

No wonder we are tired of pointing out that culture and belief arise from accidents of birth

No wonder there is no minister to regulate the supply of fear and superstition

No wonder we should decide what is acceptable and unacceptable and when we have had enough of nonsense and if we have reached that point now what next

No wonder eternity is neither here nor there since in a few million years man's presence on this earth will be a thin line of carbon in the strata and no one there to see it

No wonder absurdity gives rise to joy

No wonder we are not afraid

Ocean's edge

In an empty swimming pool
stripping the bottom of old paint
with a flaring water jet
flashing flaky bits away
man's work is often thus
violent noisy tedious
when I awoke and saw
the seething watery blade
by scouring weaker places first
had formed an archipelago
of scattered islands in a tidal bay
Celebes Java and a Borneo
emerged beneath the spray
and stayed a million years or so
changing and diminishing until
they vanished in the undertow.

Along the far west coast of Ireland
best seen from high up in the air
the final shore before America
fingers of land reach into the sea
fingers of sea reach into the land
the green is merging into blue
from high above you can't tell where
land becomes sea or ceases to be land
do you remember when you and I were there
near Bantry or Dingle down by the very water
and watched the Atlantic sucking at the rocks
indeed we threw a pebble in the ocean
to speed the process up.

On the perception of space in the Los Angeles freeway system

We are listening to directions at the rental car depot
we need to know the best route out of town we oughta go
to head for Arizona we will need the I-15
it looks real close and easy half an inch from where we been.
OK the man is saying right outa here you make a right
you want Manchester avenue and at the third stop light
you make another right keep lookin right and when you seen
the sign for I-10 south it take you down to I-15.

Appreciate we drawl in all-American style welcome
says he but I not taking in the numerous random
and other rights was wondering at word shapes in the air
as he was speaking and what Manchester was doing there.
We hit the gas and surge away we are gliding in our car
we know this what we voted for and why we went to war
this is beyond pleasure this the democratic system
citizens are cruising by appreciating freedom.

We have screwed it up already two rights have made a wrong
another right should make a square and get us back along
the street we started from this dumb naive Euclidean view
of space which works out on a sheet of paper isn't true.
We had it reasoned out we thought we'd make a quick traverse
but all the streets went on too long the angles were perverse
and when we took a hopeful right it worked out in reverse
and gave a novel proof of the expanding universe.

We found when turning into lesser streets and roads confined
within still smaller areas and obviously defined
in terms of the periphery we had just driven round
the contents of such unknown zones are not by edges bound.
We have arrived in mapless space and we are travelling
in moving holes which keep expanding and unravelling
each time we shift the gear we shift the relativities
as places leak beyond their limits in Los Angeles.

Now we have all but given up on finding the best route
in fact we're slightly crazed since geometry has spat us out
and given us a close-up opportunity to view
half-interesting roads such as Lavinia avenue:
with no apparent end but every mile in side extensions
we drift by shopping malls of astronomical dimensions
sometimes we glimpse mysterious parallels but now we're smart
we know there's no way on this level to get back to the start.

Now pay attention we are coming to the city line
which line which city sure we missed the rightful exit sign
and sure we're hoping for another sign we're still perplexed
because we only want to get from one state to the next.
Ahead of us the traffic is being waved down to a stop
some guy up there went crazy says a charitable cop
I guess he missed his turn you lookin for I-10 I fear
there aint no way at least today of getting there from here.

Oh yes there is we make a sudden left to take us through
an unexpected hole in space and leave behind the blue
celestial flashing light here comes the warm commercial glow
around the shopping malls to guide us where we want to go.

Out of thin air

A hot clear day, cloudless –
or almost, as will be seen,
a view across the Malvern Hills,
the women are having another rest
when we all say look!
– a little fleck of white appears
above the far horizon
against the blue blue sky
where nothing was before;
another and another fleck of white
form and flow together
into a cluster and make
a cloud! – a tiny cloud,
no bigger than your hand;
now the little cloud
swims slowly sideways
in a convection of the air,
breaks up and disappears
while back above the hill
a new white spot is born.

We saw this once in Spain amid
the shimmering arid lands, we thought
it took the crucible of the south
to start a cloud laboratory.
The void is full of elements
condensing sometimes into clouds;
I thought of words appearing unexpected
out of thin air where there were none before,
if not kept they scatter to the wind
and pop and vanish in oblivion.
Sublimity evaporates:
people lose interest,
we all go home for a glass of wine
in a chilled and cloudy glass.

Outsiders

We are travelling in a strange cold country;
we seem at an extreme, even the train
around a corner hangs upon the void
and delivers us in clouds of breath upon the air.
Beside the road the snowed-up forest starts,
thick and solid along the river bank;
after that the map is white with emptiness.
There is nothing cruel about a land in winter,
it is full of life continuing, and merely cold,
so cold you might promptly sleep for ever
unless you have a man or dog to lie against.
Desperate trappers clung to rocky shores,
traded their very lives between the tribes,
knew fear of death, were saved by indians
who shared their seeds and pelts and women
until they knew the uses of the frozen land.
What does collective memory mean
of peoples here for twenty thousand years,
the habits of the place, the cold in winter,
the mosquitoes in summer, the distances,
the precautions before everything unknown.
Absurdity shames the transient visitors,
the outsiders, the casual onlookers, the seekers
after extremes, the raconteurs in warm places,
the curious travellers only half-aware
that knowledge in the apparent wilderness
was laid down patiently in life after life
making an unseen mark upon the empty map.

Pale and waving

She bobs and ducks and smiles
her face comes sideways close to mine
she bends in curves to speak
she is telling a strange tale
which I can hardly follow
distracted by the motion
imagining her body pale and waving
like an anemone in strong waters.

Children are dodging everywhere
this is a birthday in the village hall
men in tee shirts drinking pints
the band is playing retro Elvis
they are called the Wild Roadies
they are old and blooming loud
the host comes by we nod and jiggle
meaning fine and how are you.

Her neighbour picked her up and shook her
pulled up a dozen trees of theirs
their landrover burnt behind the pub
it is because they live up near the cross
I don't say but it is strange up there
something unholy about the place
the people are erratic and crooked
like the trees there twisted in the wind.

We applaud a solo keyboard riff
our host had joined the band nodding
and grinning in Ray Charles shades
while she emptied her story out
her gestures have died away
she is shrivelling and closing up
swaying and apologising and we
are shuffling round and moving on.

Pear-shaped

S
t
r
ange
expressions creep
up on you it seems funny
that when things fail they go
pear-shaped who first said this
and when you hear it in pubs
where young men say their
project has gone it can it
be scientific like a drop of
water dropping or cultural
like when the cartoon cat
fetches up with a bulbous
splat! now it is a popular
phrase you don't see people
looking puzzled if they hear it
except my mother would had she
not passed away before she heard it
she was that kind of unworldly person she
would have smiled pleasantly not wanting to
offend through incomprehension once famously
in about 1957 she called a neighbour an old sod in an
innocent sort of way my father and I looked at one another
smiling saying you can't say that mother he who had been in the war
knew such things I who was a teenager knew such things now I want the
pleasure of saying this or that is going pear-shaped this poem for example it
seems a good surreal transformation and I like pears as well unfortunately I fear
the expression may be a shameful sexist slur insulting to women as if pear-shaped
is undesirable personally I disagree I have known and loved fabulous pear shapes
lying on a pear shape is much better than on an apple or a prune in which case I
have earned the right to say it however some people dismiss the sexist view
because they think the drôle idea comes from Erik Satie's composition
Trois pièces en forme de poire except there aren't three pieces
there are seven but millions of English-speaking
working people saying pear-shaped
in pubs don't know this
yet

Peter Pan

On a cold war Sunday morning
in a big coat against the chill
walking in Kensington Gardens
down a particular path
for the first and only time
saw people pausing by a statue
it was Peter Pan of course
when I by accident
colliding with a man
performed a pirouette
apologising but he tugged down
his revolutionary cap
dodged my words and leapt away
it was Nureyev of course.

Poet swept away

A symmetrical round hill,
a muted green volcanic cone
transformed by arduous effort
into a terraced ziggurat,
a mountain or a monument
of unrecorded labour and decay.
The women raked, the boys brought stones,
the men appraising rock by rock
enmeshed the walls, locked bulging earth
with keystones in the mountainside.
In the chambers of the mountain
secret water stands and builds.

At the greatest lower terrace wall
a poet has come to read out loud.
After a page or two he pauses,
listens and taps upon the stone:
there is a noise inside the mountain,
he has never heard its like before
nor will again: the mountain groans.
A keystone trembles and protrudes,
as long as half a man it pushes forth
as shaken wine expels a cork;
the wall swells out and bursts
a spout of water shoots
the bank in slurry flows
and higher slopes are splitting too.
All the water in the mountain
has been flushed out, a torrent
tears past towards the sea,
the mud coagulates in drifts.
The poet is found wallowing in slime,
a small green frog reciting in his ear;
in the valley now new light, new time,
the mountainside swept smooth and clear.

Portrait of Hans Bollebakker

When you meet up with him again
his eyes flash behind his glasses
his teeth glint within his beard
his arms enwrap you in a whiskery way.

Then straight to business.
From the refrigerator come
the fillets of herring, barely supple,
and young jenever, ultra supple.

We have the photo when he helped
the dear companion of his life
transport a full-grown emu up the street,
mistaken for a standard lamp.

This is a man who saves old buildings,
who establishes the history
and quality of heritage because
he has the metaphors within himself.

We walk with Hans around the town,
stopping to pay respects in front
of various old friends, and all
of them extremely well preserved.

Redheugh Bay
for Brigit and Chris

Behind the house the garden falls away,
the sea will scoop the whole lot out one day.
Let's slither down the slope until we reach
the empty stretches of the glistening beach.

Empty? this beach is full of salty pleasures,
like broken bottles polished into treasures,
or useful driftwood or small creatures' bones,
and we as usual are picking stones.

The stones! they're more like galaxies or brains
smoothed by the sea in whorls of red brown grains.
But nothing brought them here; they are from here,
they are the beach's fruit carved out each year.

Oh, leave the pebbles for another day,
the sea will wash them when we go away.
We're nearly at the flat bit now, hurray!
It was fifty years ago... it is today.

Remembering Beirut

Poor words poor words
falling in the howling air
like bodies uncounted
eyes hands mouths scattered
mixed up with earth
after rain the desert blooms
around the accidental tombs.

Children playing in the ruins
dynamite bursts stone
stone blunts scissors
scissors cut paper
ah but paper wraps dynamite
we played in ruins too
once upon a time
it is what children like to do.

Words form into a mass
into a rolling ball
like warrior ants
to cross a river
or pass through fire
as if an idea might gain force
meanwhile the planet
is whirling us around
children ruins altogether
in a blur unseen
blue green blue green.

Revulsion

being words from a review on the front page of a bygone issue of Poetry News

great delicacy
undeniable toughness
detailed domesticity
lyrical beauty
brave and honest
pain and rage
metaphor of memory
haunting tenderness
not sentimental
deeply moving
risk and dare
iridescent sheen
magical surface
devastating depth
muscular and delicate
plangent bitter music
twists hybrid colours
rich sensual
perfectly controlled
memory and loss
subverted tensions
innocence and experience
sense of wonder
sense of revulsion
painful and tedious

Routine exercise

~ To make some space and save on storage costs we decided to discard our old financial records, in a routine exercise.

~ Our auditors advised that records more than six years old need not be retained.

~ The obvious method was to take the papers to the recycling centre, but we did not wish to see our bank statements and company transactions all blowing in the wind.

~ After considering a shredder, which we did not have, I undertook to burn the records on the bonfire in my garden.

~ At the warehouse I collected fourteen bankers' boxes of old papers, taped up and filthy, and put them in my truck, filling the load space at the back and everywhere inside except the driver's seat.

~ Upon the bonfire place I built two towers of papers four feet high and leaning together for stability, and poured petrol on the piles.

~ I stepped back and threw a match, the towers ignited in a series of whumping noises as reservoirs of fuel were found.

~ The wind blew strongly across the flaring papers and fragments still burning, curling, disintegrating, streamed away in the dancing air.

~ The piles of papers began to lean and fold until they collapsed and spilled outwards across the ground.

~ The burning became a nibbling at the edges of the blocks of paper while the wind continually blew off the ashy residue and reddened the advancing surface.

~ There emerged a new profile of our bank statements, recast and rounded like an arch of narrow medieval bricks or the strata of an upturned cliff once scoured by the sea.

~ Now the mass of papers smoothed by fire and wind has taken on the form of a fallen man, there is the head, back and legs, grey and quivering with heat, bent round and lying in a foetal position, like one of the moulds at Pompeii, cast from a void in the volcanic ash where the person was overwhelmed.

~ I was impatient with this natural process and took the rake and stirred the smouldering heaps to flame, running after half-burnt sheets, eyes streaming in the smoke, seeing the ideas, profits, names and efforts of years gone by scattered into drifting ghosts.

Secrets of the body

Thinking of a hilltop settlement
in Provence or Italy
I am perching comfortably
upon a warm divided monument;
grasping with both hand and eye
the landscape's smooth convexity
the transitory swerving step
from back and waist toward the hip;
thinking of some country formula
for drizzling olive oil on fresh ciabatta
watching evening light move across the skin
and fade where darker areas begin.

Now drip the shining oil
unctuously into the small
of your back and so create
a pool in a sleepy hollow;
then sweep it down below
and with a finger irrigate
the warm cleavage where
slow leviathan has stirred
and presses nearer
one or other of its lairs.

Stones

Not sharp or broken
or in a pathetic way
ugly and unbalanced –
who feels sorry for a stone –
but smooth sculpturous forms
scoured by an ocean of time;
weights that sit in the hand
like a hard puppy,
shapes that swell and develop
and go back in and round;
those holes waiting in stone
hard to believe but useful
to pass a rope through
to make a weight or an object.

The hillside path, itself
a torrent of stone,
this seabed, this lagoon,
this pool of darting shrimps
lifted slowly into sunlight
an inch in a thousand years,
bleached and greened, now
flies and lizards flicker
over heat-blown pebbles;
stranded caves remember
in the precipice
the feel of water;
down the mountain track
rocks are brought by truck,
complex, heavy, ravined,
dripping with ants,
now set upon the terrace,
worth turning over
to see the other face of the moon
worth the satisfaction

the muscular effort
of heaving the blind lump.

He ponders small curiosities,
individual stones acquire function
become utensil/paperweight/ashtray,
painted egg or robin;
phallus-like or vulva travel secretly upstairs;
among the pale hard bright objects
here is a stone of maternal warmth;
another like his father, brittle,
the first he will later break;
here is a former mistress,
smoothish on the palm,
a disappointment once turned over;
himself, self always in them all,
universal dust imagined for a while
burst from a volcano or from
the chalk of creatures pressed
and flung away.

On a night full of full moon
he taps one stone upon another;
taking the most potent pebble
to smash its glistening family;
inspecting the petrified insides
for the look of ancient time;
tentatively, experimentally,
unaware of sharp or hard,
of himself or other,
he cuts indifferently;
and lies panting, absolved,
in a crimson pool
upon the fragmentary debris
waiting for the vast white stars
to cover all in dust.

Tamara speaks

acknowledging a page in The Guardian, *c.2003, of mugshots of individuals subsequently executed.**

We cannot stare into Tamara's eyes
though on that day they glistened terribly;
we only see a page, an inky print,
a copy of a fragile photograph
made of decaying chemicals once saved
in darkness in a file for fifty years
now found and resurrecting casually
a woman caught before the camera's eye.

The ghost has shadowed lines at lip and brow
held tight in irony and self-defence;
disdaining fantasy, Tamara speaks:
– in a few moments when you throw my corpse
upon a truck amid the morning's works,
remember, savour in your mouths not just
the smell of blood but knowledge that one day
your lives will end in fear and decay.

Now other staring faces form and seem
to speak – Aziz: for certain I was purged
because I was a muslim beekeeper;
bearded Dionis: because I was a monk;
weeping Ruzya: because I spoke my mind
yet left no message for my family;
smiling Victor: because I don't know why.
Speak to them now, in case the spirit hears!
We wake too late, and comfort disappears.

* See David King: *Ordinary Citizens: the Victims of Stalin.* London, 2003.

The burning cave

On a mountain in the night
I dreamt that three of us
were sitting in a stony place
upon the ground before
a cavern full of fire.
She, my companion,
resting on my right
and on the other side
a younger man unknown
and yet familiar.
He smiles
and standing straight
strips off his robe
steps naked
into the burning cave;
we see him slowly
moving deeper
until he grows bright
and vanishes in light.
I am afraid to follow
although I know
a life untested
remains unproved.
Or was it a shadow self
detached from me
to show the way.

The enormous waft

– dinner soon his mother says
– just round the block he says
briskly he is away
past friends' houses past the stables
past the pig farm with no pigs
past where round the block would go
intently the boy is walking
sees scuffed schoolboy shoes
knees grey socks
come forward with each step

on the grassgrown bridge he waits
hears the rails begin to sing
at the very moment leaning
on his chest across the parapet
looks right down the funnel –
and ducks back double quick
before the next enormous waft
of smoke embalms his face
– done it! he says
and feels a drop of rain

steadily he walks he spurns to run
it is pouring now he sees
his scuffed shoes kicking puddles
he pulls his lumber jacket collar up
his favourite he is snug
he feels wonderful
he knows he is alive
part of him watches from above
back home he gets told off
because he is late and wet

The flow of water

After rain,
in the field beyond my house
a stream came to the surface.

With a spade
I went there to examine
and encourage the new flow.

The water
is bubbling from the grass! I am midwife
to a newly risen Amazon.

With a pulse
and tiny rippling noise, clear pools form
and flow across my fingers.

While it flowed
I hoped for a torrent, but the weather dried:
the stream sank back beneath the earth.

Rivers sink
from sight, making deeper channels in the dark,
scouring unseen cathedrals.

Strange creatures
move pale and eyeless and unknown
in the reservoirs below.

In hard times
knowledge shrivels, false blossoms sprout
in gaudy colours out of poisoned wells.

The river
re-emerging may have spent a thousand years
within its secret chambers.

Remember
the flow of water on your fingers, before
the stream is covered by the earth once more.

The long dark place

I must have woken and found myself
in blackness so thick and solid
it weighed upon my face; I know
I stretched my arm out in the dark
as far as I could reach and touched
nothing, as if there were nothing there,
and with a shiver brought my hand
back into bed and warm and safe.
This was my earliest memory.

I knew I was brought down sometimes
asleep and put beneath the stairs,
I knew the long dark place was where
the stairs come down to meet the ground.
At the other side, on other nights,
I would have seen a line of light
and heard my mother's voice as she
drank tea among the bottled jams
in the so-called air raid shelter.
So flimsy was it, never mind a bomb,
a hammer would have knocked it down.
A bomb did fall around that time,
jettisoned beside the Liverpool road,
erasing by chance the memories
of a family we didn't know.

The muse escapes

After Stevie Smith's poem: Who is this who howls and mutters?

It shifts and whispers as it waits,
scratching and lapping at the boards,
the muffled tide behind the door.

Otherwise comfortable in here,
the usual table, lamp and chair,
books and pictures on the wall.

Fear of a stinking brackish swell
with worms and leeches on the skin,
repulsive fertile clouds of spawn.

At the horizon horses fall,
a fort besieged in gold and blue,
in the city perfervid talk.

A clear fresh torrent bursting through
carries off table, chair and all,
the landscape is a shining lake
where papers drift and disappear.

The road from melancholy

i.m. Michael Donaghy, d. 2004. References are to his collection Errata *and to Keats'* Ode on Melancholy.

No, no... go not to Liverpool, nor search along the Mersey
shore,
the tattooing shack is boarded and graffiti'ed o'er;
the girls behind Pierhead and down the Scottie Road
got dressed and all went home for tea or motherhood.
Don't think of shadowing the shebeens of Sligo
or questioning the fiddler in Flanagan's, Chicago;
up in the Bronx the nightly burning fire escapes
have long since cauterised footprints and body shapes.
Look not toward the dazzling currents of oblivion
where ghosts of men go streaming past Byzantium,
and future sounds of poems unwritten and unsung
remain among the spirit's cloudy trophies hung.
Among us here his heraldries of light are saved
in flickering words and on our memories engraved.

The roads round here

at Blauvac in Provence; translated from the author's 'Les chemins d'ici'

Go to the edge; soon
you will see them, the paths waiting
for you there, but first look
how the road from here starts off:
soon it hides and disappears
upon another level;
the road is already what it will become:
the beginning the end the continuation
of all roads.

You see you as well
are a departure and a continuation;
you see the confused tracks around us
dropping, unrolling, veering away,
crossing, starting anew, startling themselves,
sometimes reaching a dead end,
one or another, then peeling off, fleeing
to the horizon to join up again
in other realms.

Do you recognise the reflections in nature:
the vine sends tender tendrils
to build a hardening pathway
filled with fruit;
the air in imitation sends the swifts,
their dives and swoops in a single second
surpassing the twelve month of the vine;
constantly they reinvent their dazzling tracks
filled with emptiness.

Look well upon these trails of history
long-time routes of beasts of the night
crouching in the fields of ancient knowledge
following the subtle directions of the earth
tracks lent to man
just now by man made hard
filled with stones
and by the imprint of our feet and language
charged with new ideas.

We don't make new paths
we don't crush new flowers
we put our feet in the trace
of those who went before;
imagine – eyes half-closed – the roads
of empire pillage faith abandonment
and ordinary work;
of all that has been and will be again
the echos reach us.

And you, you others, crowding the roads,
who formerly met talked embraced
and sometimes killed, arise you ghosts,
how is it we see you no more
this fine summer's day like summer days of yesterday,
perhaps we would see you returning along these same paths
on a winter evening with dusk falling, yes,
we would hear the cries the muttered words the dragged heels
we would know you, our ancestors, our kin.

Look closely at the faces of the people you meet
the people sitting next to you
look well in case you see familiar features
of two thousand, one thousand years ago
or of this evening
and the voices you hear
your neighbour's voice his wife's or else your own
they are the same voices which echo along the roads
since the early time.

As for us: tomorrow and in a thousand years
people will meet on the roads round here
looking in each others' eyes and of course
they will see us they will hear us
dust clad with dust
as we have seen those we loved so well
those who have lent us their lives
the dear unknown phantoms who imbue the roads
with their whispers.

If you doubt it, go down from the village
and look around Our Lady of the Snows
where the old road slows down
ask of the shades waiting there
if you are alone or if
in your little moment you are sustained
by the slow vines
the hollow tracks of the swifts
the white dust of the roads round here.

The wind of time

It was long ago
but the wind has brought it back.
She was four years old
it was springtime and a gale blowing
we had cut trees down
to give more light, as you must know
a wood has a collective shape
the outside trees absorb the wind
but if you have them down
the inside trees are suddenly exposed.

I was inside the house
and heard the rending –
tore outside running hard
running as fast as I could
I knew where she was playing
round beyond the garage
I saw the garage
it was bisected by a tree
a cloud of dust was in the air
I came round the corner at full speed
and in the dust
beside the fallen trunk
her hands up near her face
my daughter stood
in her bobbly jumper
her little cart a yard away
beneath the tree.

Where I live today
an autumn gale is blowing.
From the oak tree
it has dislodged
some branches for the fire.
Sometimes I imagine
tearing outside again

running as fast as I can
around the corner
into the cloud of dust
and this time see
the bobbly jumper
underneath the tree.

Later I might go
and visit the woman
who has all but forgotten
the story of the tree
and look at her
and hold her hands
and wonder how to understand
the slender margins
that make all the difference
or even what it is
I am trying to understand.

The wind's edge
for Drake Mabry

here was a fortress
sea sucked a tunnel through
the almost-island
ate the cliff-edge down
a kingdom too

here is the moving line
fragments rattle in the tow
the ancient heaving dance
of land and sea uncertain
where they'll go

this very pebble
was lying near
it makes a pretty
paperweight this thing
or this idea

Think about it

Come back and see me one day
there are a lot of new things going on
the way we live changes we have made
so many ideas you didn't hear about.
We could have quite different conversations
like equals with a space between us.

You'll find me different of course
so many events in work and love
some will sadden you some may please
and me harder, softer, so to speak grown up.
It would be strange to see you again
to hear your voices would be like going home.

Think about it
it's nonsense of course
I'll think about it by myself.

To the light
translated from the author's 'Vers la lumière'

walking through a meadow
along a white path
with poppies and cornflowers
to either side while on the left
there is a great rock
and you pass through it
not round but through
somehow through a cleft
and into a chamber
there seems to be light
in this chamber and all round
there are doors you can choose
a door there is one
the obvious choice ahead
and just to the right
already ajar you pass through
easily enough and then
there is a kind of corridor
curving and constricting
you cannot see
you cannot breathe
you cannot move
you want to oblige
and move on but you can't
you don't know what to do
you think you have failed

a voice says
let the light draw you on
what light you say
is there light
my eyes are closed
the voice says
make an effort for yourself
something shifts you feel
you are the swimmer the diver
arms at sides
hair plastered back
shooting up from the deep
toward the surface
then bursting through
into the light
and you weep
how you weep

Vase versus flower

Has the vase no purpose
but to hold a flower
more lovely than the vase?

If the vase is lovely
on its own account
does it need the flower?

Lumpish clay has passed through
transformation in the fire
to become a vase.

An ugly vase has been
through fire too and is
as lovely in intent.

How should we judge ourselves?
We are vessels, sometimes
we hold a flower.

If the vase is empty
shall we break the vase
because it is empty?

Written in French (A)

English people often say they love
the French language without knowing why
it is because a young couple have met
no it is out of ignorance and sentiment
all right it is because of the idea that
a young couple have met on the Pont des Arts
they will go to a hotel on the Île St-Louis
shyly he will caress her breasts and enter her;
people like words like this, perhaps later
she will find she is pregnant
and then we will all feel differently;
oh yes we enjoy enjoyable words,
and we hate hateful words especially
when he pulps a slimy mess upon her face
although he does it lovingly because
they are squashing strawberries during sex;
only the French do this, of course.

Written in French (B)

Some words suggest a colour or a scent
but not to everybody and not just
words like swart or sweat or sweltering;
the writer of words like gront or partlet
does not know if they smell nice.
There is no point in saying what
should or should not be the case since
the absurdity of words discourages
a small number of people from the effort.
Let us retreat smiling nonchalantly
and linger lounging in our lighthouses
peering into the unseen wondering
how many years before the light goes out:
while warning signs stand at the cliff edge,
the signs say or the talking ones would say,
believe nothing, test things for yourself.
These words are written in French, of course.
C'est quand-même dommage, j'aurais bien aimé...

You can't see everything

translated from the author's 'On ne peut pas tout voir'

You can't see everything
but if you go for a walk
and your companion says
did you see the fox
slipping into the vines?
did you see the snail
crawling across the leaf?
did you see the white stone
that looked like the face of god?
did you see the shooting star
that joined two worlds together?
but you saw none of these fine things
you were staring at your feet and your thoughts
you collect yourself
you say to your companion
no but you saw the fox
the snail the stone the star
you saw them for me
I saw them with your eyes
I share them
and because I don't possess them
I can love them
as I love transitory things
especially when they are far off
and when I occasionally succeed
in not crushing them with gross desire
I can learn to hover above the world
to hover
before my body finally
turns back into earth
and fox
and star

the first shall be   the last shall be   the first and last   in the parting   in the middle   in the joining   B

B

C

in the turning   turning towards   the glance ahead   turning back to   the lost moment   the remembrance   D

C

D

INSTRUCTIONS: cut along dotted lines. Attach BB to CC. Hold both ends of strip and give one end half a turn. Attach DD to AA.

A

turning we all   we all retire askew   turning they all   they all are joined anew   turning the last   the last or first

A

the present moment   the appearance   the absence then   the faces separate   the faces joined   the faces are the face